# PEARL GOURAMI 101

# GUIDES

## Pearl Gourami 101: Care, food, disease, Tank Mates, Size, And Breeding

## Heather Walter

# Table of Contents

# CHAPTER ONE

# INTRODUCTION

Pearl gouramis are a fun and extraordinary freshwater fish that we suggest frequently.

In addition to the fact that they look astounding, however thinking about them is pretty darn simple. They're solid fish who won't cause inconvenience in your tank. You can likewise keep them in sensibly measured tanks which is a need for some aquarists. Yet, there are a few things you'll have to know whether you need to assist them with living long, glad lives. This guide spreads out all the basic components of pearl gourami care to ensure possessing one is easy.

The pearl gourami (logical name: trichopodus leerii) is a freshwater maze fish that hails from Southeast Asia. It's likewise alluded to as the trim gourami and mosaic gourami by a few.

The principle nations of inception are Malaysia, Thailand, and the islands of Borneo and Sumatra in Indonesia. They've likewise been found in northern South America once in a while too (in spite of the fact that this is because of human intercession and not a characteristic relocation).

In their characteristic natural surroundings, the pearl gourami invests the majority of their energy in the top portion of whatever waterway they're in. This is regularly in acidic waters, for example, overwhelms yet they have been known to discover out to more stale feeders, low streams, and lakes every once in a while.

This fish has been a staple freshwater consideration for a long while, with reproducing proceeding to be a need inside the aquarist network. Now, it's elusive

a nation where they are anything
but a generally included decision!

## CHAPTER TWO

# LIFE EXPECTANCY AND APPEARANCE

The normal pearl gourami life expectancy is around 4-5 years. There have been accounted for cases where this fish has made it recent years old, however that is very extraordinary.

Giving the correct pearl gourami care is fundamental in the event that you need your fish to hit the upper-finish of that life expectancy go. While they're commonly simple to think about, you can abbreviate their life expectancy fundamentally on the off chance that you don't furnish them with the natural surroundings condition they need.

The "solid fish" name can some of the time lure proprietors into intuition they don't have to perspire the little stuff. In any case, consider it thusly: if your fish lives to 4 with below average consideration, it presumably would have hit 5 in ideal conditions!

## Appearance

Pearl gouramis are a novel and brilliant freshwater fish, there's no rejecting that. It's most likely the primary motivation behind why you discover them in so numerous aquariums! A great deal of fish are tough and simple to think about, yet their look truly makes them stick out.

Their name originates from the way that this fish is set apart with minimal white specks that stretch over by far most of their bodies including their caudal and dorsal blades. The main spot where you won't have the option to discover these specks is on a little fix underneath their mouth that stretches out marginally down to their paunch.

These pearl-like spots make a hypnotizing visual particularly when they're swimming. From the correct edge they nearly sparkle!

Another brand name highlight of the pearl gourami is the dark line that runs down the center of their body, beginning from their mouth and finishing toward the start of their caudal blade. The haziness of this light can differ somewhat relying upon the tinge of the remainder of the fish, however it's in every case very perceptible.

Their bodies are dainty and level however they're fairly tall and long (like the midget gourami). This gives them a smidgen of a "sideways flapjack" look while by one way or another actually looking long and quick!

Another particular quality of pearl gourami is their long and slim ventral balances. These hang while they swim and can stretch out past the finish of their caudal balances now and again. They look sort of interesting yet we believe it's an adorable look.

## Size

The normal pearl gourami size is somewhere close to 4-5 inches.

This estimation applies to their body and doesn't tally any reward length they may get from their ventral balances.

The size of this fish can be affected by various elements like :

- Genetics

- Care

- Age

- Gender

## CHAPTER THREE

# PEARL GOURAMI CARE

As we referenced before, pearl gourami care isn't actually advanced science. These fish are genuinely low-upkeep and don't need a huge amount of additional consideration, in contrast to some different species.

Notwithstanding, you totally should know the basics in the event that you need them to carry on with upbeat and solid lives. We generally urge fish proprietors to find out however much about their fish as could be expected, on the grounds that no one can tell when it will prove to be useful later on.

## Tank Size

The suggested least tank size for pearl gourami is 30 gallons. Some consideration aides may disclose to you that you can pull off 20, yet that is excessively little as we would see it.

Utilizing 30 gallons as the beginning stage will give your fish a lot of space to investigate and research any of the plants and shakes that you've included.

In the event that you plan on keeping more than one pearl gourami you should include around 5-10 additional gallons for each fish.

## Water Parameters

The suggested water boundaries for pearl gourami is something that many individuals misconstrue. Ideally this puts any misinformation to rest.

• Water temperature: 77°F to 82°F

- pH levels: 6.5 to 8

- Water hardness: 5-25 dH

## What To Put In Their Tank

With the end goal for you to recreate their regular environment however much as could reasonably be expected, there are a couple of things you'll need to add to their tank.

The first is plants. Pearl gourami originate from waterways that are exceptionally wealthy in vegetation, so it's something they expect causes them to feel great.

It's only normal for them to collaborate with plants.

They're not known to be enormous plant-eaters so you have a great deal of choices with regards to the sort of plants you need to incorporate. Hornwort is a typical decision just as Brazilian waterweed, yet don't hesitate to explore different avenues regarding anything!

Rocks are another extraordinary thing to remember for their tank. The low waters and marshes where pearl gouramis originate from are brimming with them, so this is another simple method to cause things to feel like home.

Logs and driftwood are likewise a smart thought on the off chance that you have space. These should lay on a sandy substrate also. We know some aquarists who pull off more unpleasant substrates, however it's not suggested.

## Normal Diseases

The pearl gourami is a really sturdy animal varieties that isn't inclined to a scope of illnesses like some different sorts of fish. In any case, there is one infection that appears to torment this fish more than any others, and that malady is blade decay.

Balance decay is a bacterial infection that outcomes in harmed or spoiling tissue on the balances of your fish (duh). It will quite often begin at the very edges of the blade before working its direction internal. Whenever left untreated, it can advance right down to the base of the influenced blade.

While it is conceivable to treat balance decay in pearl gourami, it's far simpler to keep it from happening by and large. The primary driver of this infection is helpless water quality.

However long you're determined about checking levels, performing water changes, and observing your fish, it's impossible that this will influence your pearl gourami.

## CHAPTER FOUR

# FOOD AND DIET

Pearl gouramis are omnivores which gives you a ton of alternatives with regards to their eating routine. The primary concern to zero in on is balance and a comprehension of their suggested healthful admission since they'll eat basically anything.

In their normal living space, these fish will nibble on a great deal of creepy crawlies and other protein-rich food sources like eggs and green growth. They're likewise totally fine with snacking on plants on the off chance that it makes them excited.

With regards to their eating regimen in imprisonment you'll need to ensure they have a decent base of fish food from pelles or piece food. Any believed food is fine.

It's likewise brilliant to blend in some live food. This won't just give them an excellent wellspring of protein however it will give advancement to them also. Live food is an extraordinary method to trigger chasing senses which decreases feelings of anxiety (it's additionally amusing to watch).

Some great live food choices are:

- Brine shrimp

- Bloodworms

- Black worms

- Glass worms

You should try not to overload your pearl gourami since they'll keep on scarfing down anything you put in the tank. Focus on a few feedings for every day.

Likewise, watch them while they eat (particularly right off the bat) and in the event that you see a ton of food getting missed, dial back the sum. Uneaten food will become natural waste which can have a truly negative effect on the nature of your water, and raise alkali levels also.

## Behavior and Temperament

Probably the best thing about pearl gourami is their smooth personality. These are quiet fish all in all and can coexist with a wide scope of other amphibian critters.

The one time that this fish can be inclined to animosity is during the rearing or mating measure. This happens essentially with the guys, however you'll see that the female pearl gourami will act more tense also.

Like different gouramis, these fish have a maze organ which they use to relax. It works basically like a lung, which implies they have to visit the surface occasionally so as to get air.

Along these lines, you'll regularly observe your pearl gourami investing the vast majority of their energy in the upper portion of your tank. Remember this in the event that you plan on adding drifting plants to your aquarium. You would prefer not to hinder their way to oxygen!

## Pearl Gourami Tank Mates

Because of their quiet personality, the rundown of viable pearl gourami tank mates is fairly long. They can impart a tank to little fish or enormous fish as long as their tank mates aren't known to be forceful.

Pearl gourami won't start quarrel (except if it's generating time) so you'll practically never need to stress over them stumbling into difficulty in your tank.

Rather than rattling off each conceivable tank mate that is viable with pearl gourami, it bodes well for us to show a portion of the regular decisions. This will give you a decent beginning stage, and in the event that you have a fish that isn't on the rundown you can utilize the overall rules to advise your choice.

- Neon tetras

- Dwarf gourami

- Cory catfish

- Kuhli loaches

- Danios

- Cherry thorns

- Bristlenose pleco

This is simply starting to expose reasonable tank mates for your pearl gourami, yet it's a decent spot to begin.

In case you're thinking about fish outside of this rundown there are two principle things to remember to decide possible similarity.

The first is size. Regardless of whether they're tranquil, fish that are essentially bigger than your pearl gourami can make them feel dangerous and invest a ton of their energy sequestered from everything. This will prompt an expansion in feelings of anxiety and an absence of advancement.

Since they need to go to the surface to breath, they will be frightened each time!

The second is hostility. Any fish that tends to be forceful won't make a decent tank mate for pearl gourami.

Pearl gourami are an animal categories that likes to sandbar than all alone. We generally suggest that you get a couple of these fish if feasible for the accompanying reasons:

- They'll be more joyful and more advanced

- It looks astounding when a lot of them swim around the tank!

- Breeding

- Breeding pearl gourami is somewhat unique in relation to different types of fish due to how they make their homes and mate.

- The measure looks a bit of something like this:

- The guys blow bubbles that are blended in with spit that buoy to the surface. These will regularly wind up held up into different vegetation which keeps them set up

Printed in Great Britain
by Amazon

51419619R00018